My Name Is EzelL

Gayle Nelson

Copyright © 2012 Gayle Nelson

All rights reserved.

ISBN: 0615647073
ISBN-13: 978-0615647074

DEDICATION

For the Mothers of Haiti.
This book is for you –
from one mother to another.

ACKNOWLEDGMENTS

Every year in October, **Walden's Global Day of Service** showcases the wonderful things Walden students are accomplishing through a Higher Purpose Mission which encourages social change. http://servicenetwork.waldenu.edu/

100% of the proceeds of this book go to the **Humanitarian Focus Foundations** - *Building a Stronger Community*. http://humanitarianfocus.org/. The *Lire Project* focuses on providing a learning environment for Haitian children to promote improved reading skills. The curriculum emphasizes the shaping of character through the teaching of core virtues: respect, honesty, responsibility, openness and perseverance.

MY NAME IS **EZELL**.
HERE IS MY STORY.

I was walking in the woods along the mountain trail one sunny morning.

I am 7. I am very happy.

I felt the earth move and my feet slipped.

I was

    falling

        falling

            down

                down.

I was so scared.

Many days passed

I think.

I got up.

What happened?

...then I saw a white light.

So warm.

So bright.

So peaceful.

The light surrounded me then became a part of me inside me.

I saw 2 little girls crying.

Their home was gone.
They were sad.

When I touched them on their shoulder,
they turned to look at me and smiled.

People were helping them.
They were not alone.

I saw a mother standing,
looking in the distance.

She was trying to understand
even just a little portion
of all the big changes made
in just a few short seconds.

Her life was different now.

How could I help them?

I had to help them!

I bent down and started picking up rocks.

One rock at a time.

One stone at a time.

When I looked up again,
I saw a village.

>A happy village.
>A strong village.

One stone at a time.

Hand-in-hand.
Side-by-side.

ONE person

With one person

With one person

With one person makes

ONE united strong bond.

Bigger than ONE.

Stronger than ONE.

Yet ONE now.

ONE is a never-ending circle
– of People
– of Seasons.

ONE is OPEN.

Call on me.

I am there <u>always</u> to listen to you,

To help you,

To fill you with warmth.

I am patiently waiting.

You <u>know</u> I am there.

I love you.

-EzelL

The story behind **My Name is Ezell**

Walden's degree is more than education and certification and not about my work or my profession. For me it is truly about a "higher purpose." We are here right now to give. We are here right now to serve. We are here to use the gifts we have been given for the benefit of others. When we all share our gifts we complete the process, complete each other, and complete ourselves. Thank you Walden for knowing what is important. Thank you Dear Lord for showing me my higher purpose.

For decades as an artist I have looked at objects and people and drawn or portrayed what was before me. My mind took the lines and the shapes and the colors and mimicked this onto paper or whatever art form I was working. This book is about a whole new way of "seeing" – an inward glimpse. It is about stepping out on that limb and having the faith that the end product was meant to be and exactly as it should be. This book was given to me… a gift to others… an inner look and not from my thoughts or from art and education. Ezell is from a source where the lines on the paper will connect with the viewer and provide more insight for that next person. We all have gifts. Get away from our noisy world, find a peaceful place to sit down, to rest, to listen to the voices of nature, and listen to your inner voice. It will set you on the path you were meant to be on and free your soul to do what it was meant to do.

Here is the story behind this little book, *My Name is Ezell*. I am working with a wonderful fellow Walden student, Andrise Bass. During my residency with Walden, Ms. Bass was one of the featured speakers relaying to us her efforts for the Haitian peoples (andrise@humanitarianfocus.org). After the residency we exchanged emails December of 2011, she looked at my website and asked me to write a book. She was the impetus and our humble project began. Below is an excerpt from my Feb 2012 email to Andrise:

"Here is how this message came to be. I heard one morning on the radio on my way to work (up an hour earlier than usual) a program of how one writer was more or less "given" the story - the closest I can relate this to is like a channel of some sort. Then I heard "This is how I want you to do the children's book. Don't think, just write." So I decided to start this project that coming Thursday. Now I am comfortable with my art, but not the writing part necessarily... I sat down in my chair in my quiet cabin in the woods and started writing. The words just came to me ... "My name is Ezell and here is my story..." Later when I looked up the meaning of Ezell (I thought it sounded French), it was Hebrew and means *Strength of God*. Wow! I wouldn't say I am a religious woman, but I am spiritually-oriented. I believe this is the story of a little boy (or is this a Higher Being?) who was in the middle of the earthquake and passes onto another place of light - he is a messenger of some sort. But the book is for the mothers of Haiti to read to their children. To heal the mothers and heal the children. This is not from me, but from something given to me and I gladly pass it on. I am not familiar with the geography of Haiti so didn't know there were mountains while writing this. When I started to do the illustrations, I looked at photos of my grandchildren. They are multi-race dark-skinned and look much like the children of Haiti so they were my "models" more or less. I started with my granddaughter Amara's photo. I am very good at catching the exact likeness in a portrait and have done dozens here locally over the past decades, but what came out as a finished product was not a 7 year old girl in the photo, but a 30-something mother. Then, when I looked at my grandson's photo, what I drew was yes a 7 year old boy, but it was not Mehkai. It was Ezell. I am not sure if this little boy is real, or was real, but I do know his story needs to be told. "

Later, when I really started looking into the Haitian earthquake, it rang a bell with me and I looked back for the exact Thursday I was told to sit down and write this little book. It was the 2 year anniversary of the earthquake in Haiti.

Haitian mothers – this book is for you – from one mother to another. It will help us all heal. love, g

www.ingramcontent.com/pod-product-compliance
Lightning Source LLC
Chambersburg PA
CBHW041756040426
42446CB00001B/62